Anitra's Dance
from Peer Gynt Suite No.1

Edvard Grieg

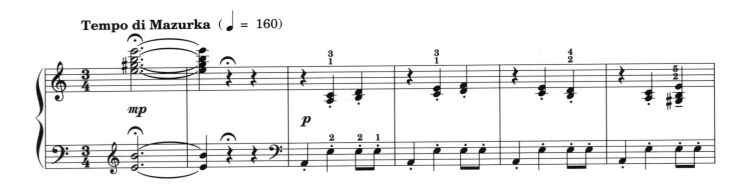

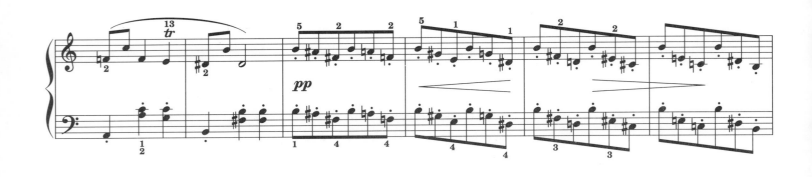

* Trills without afterbeat.

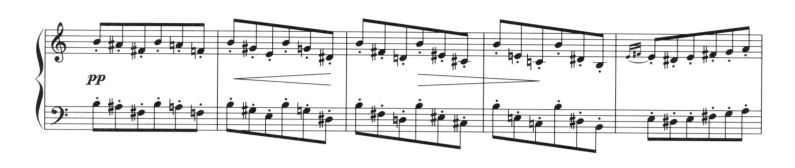

Åse's Death
from Peer Gynt Suite No.1

Edvard Grieg

Andante doloroso ($\quad$ = 80)

Album Leaf
from Lyric Pieces, Op.12

Edvard Grieg

Elegy
from Lyric Pieces, Op.38

Edvard Grieg

Allegretto semplice ♩ = 80

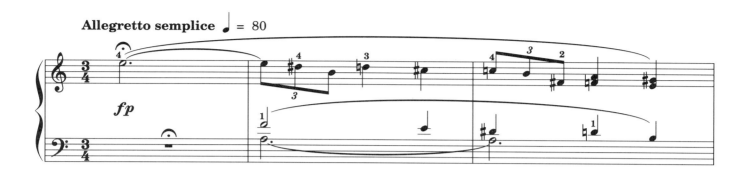

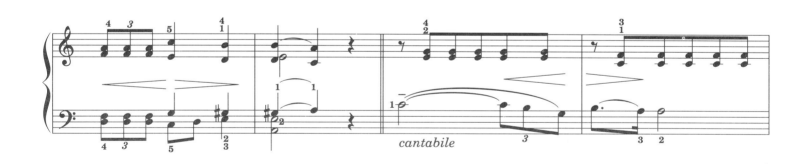

Elves Dance
from Lyric Pieces, Op.12

Edvard Grieg

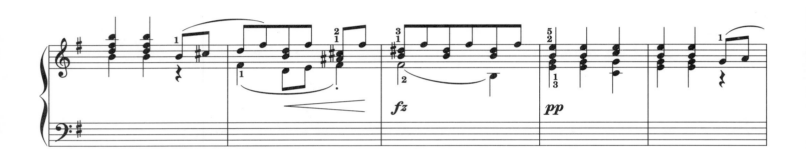

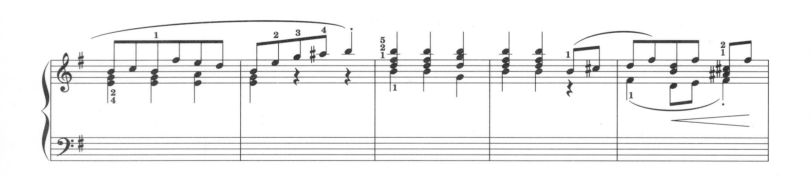

Evening In The Mountains
from Lyric Pieces, Op.68

Edvard Grieg

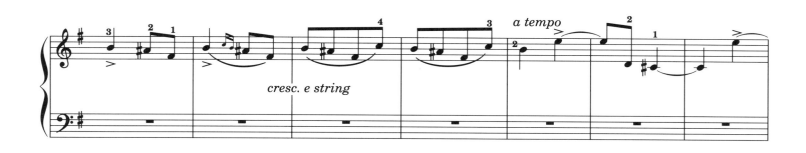

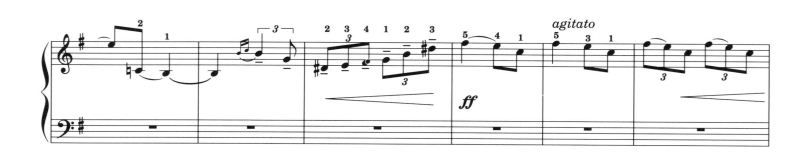

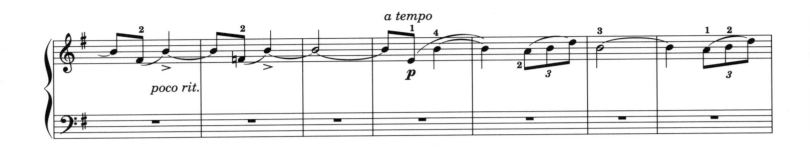

20

21

Gavotte
from The Holberg Suite

Edvard Grieg

23

Musette
Un poco più mosso

Gavotte da Capo al Fine

24

Homesickness
from Lyric Pieces, Op.57

Edvard Grieg

Molto più vivo

pp una corda

poco rit.

28

poco a poco più lento al Fine

rit.

In My Homeland
from Lyric Pieces, Op.43

Edvard Grieg

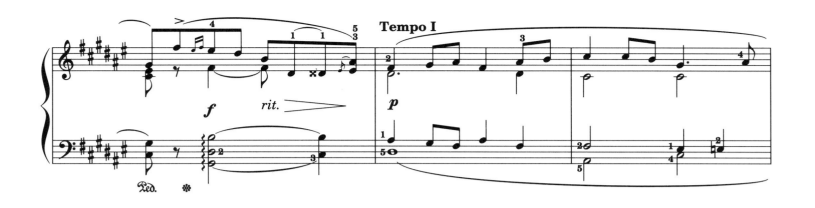

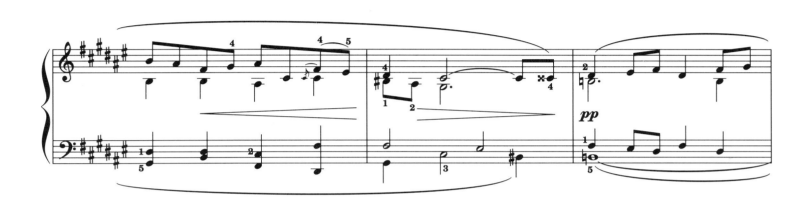

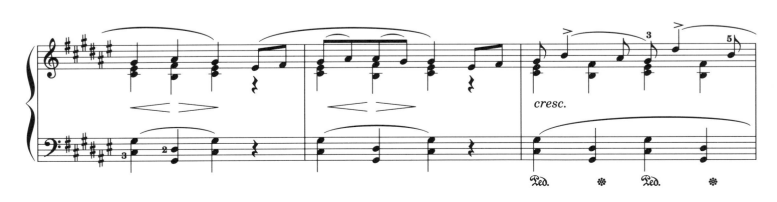

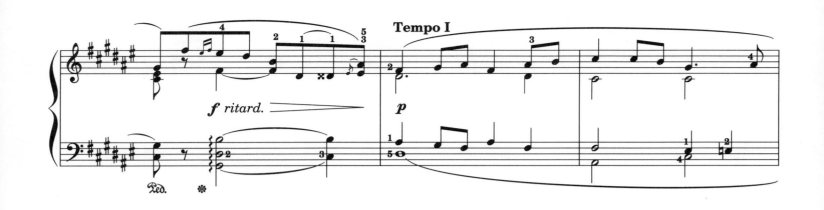

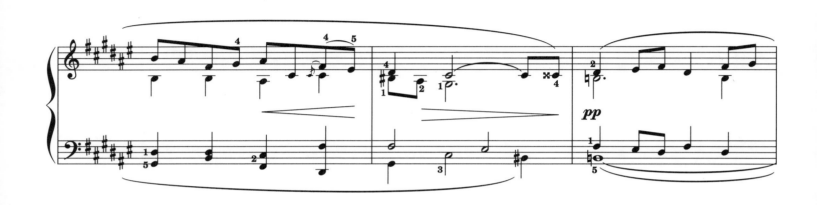

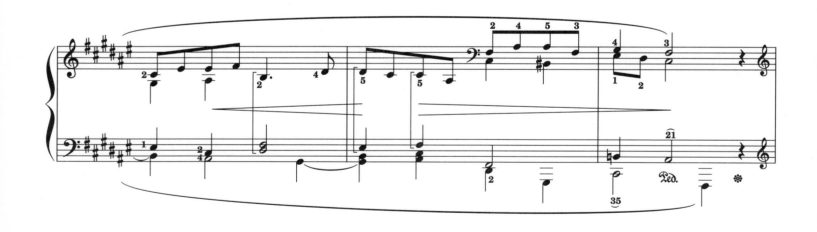

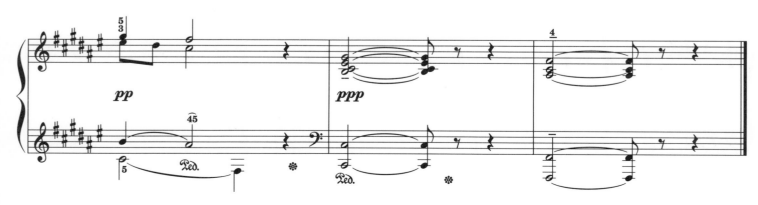

Melody
from Lyric Pieces, Op.47

Edvard Grieg

Allegretto

34

Leaping Dance
from Lyric Pieces, Op.38

Edvard Grieg

Morning Mood
from Peer Gynt Suite No.1

Edvard Grieg

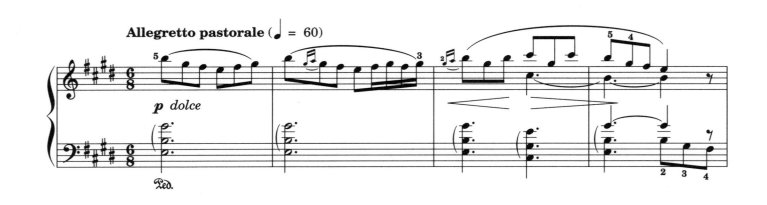

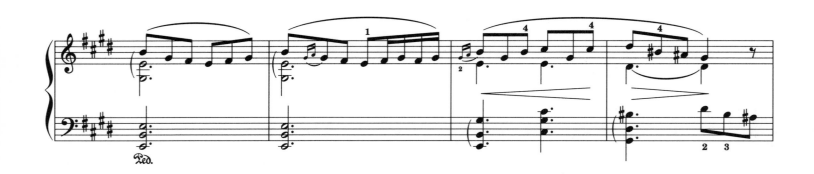

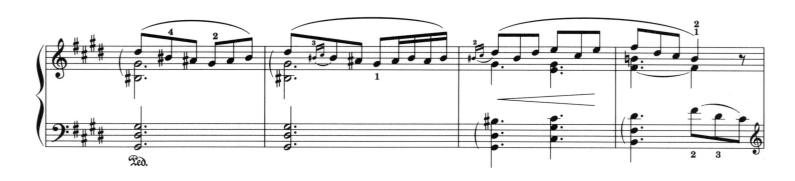

41

43

Peasants' March
from Lyric Pieces, Op.54

Edvard Grieg

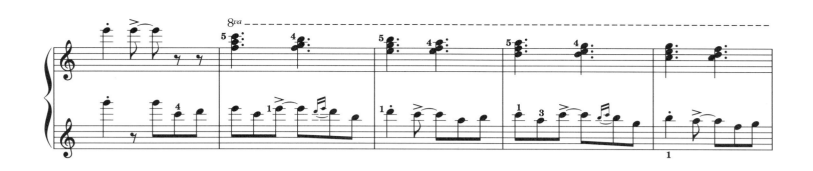

50

Sarabande
from The Holberg Suite

Edvard Grieg

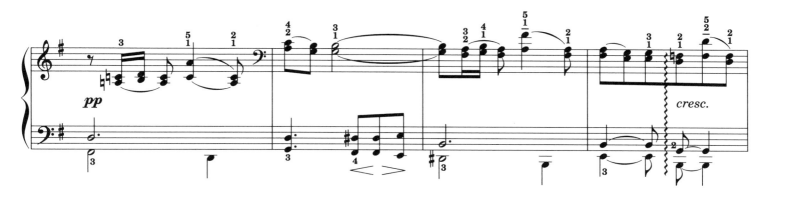

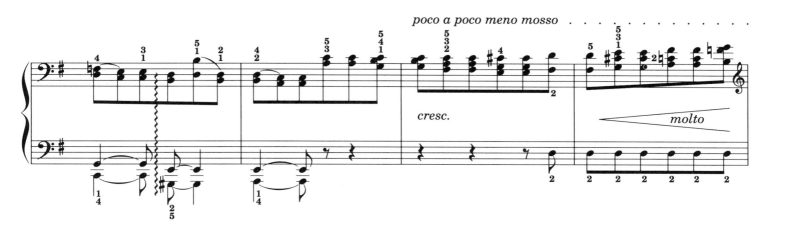

poco a poco meno mosso . . . .

Tempo I

Shepherd Boy
from Lyric Pieces, Op.54

Edvard Grieg

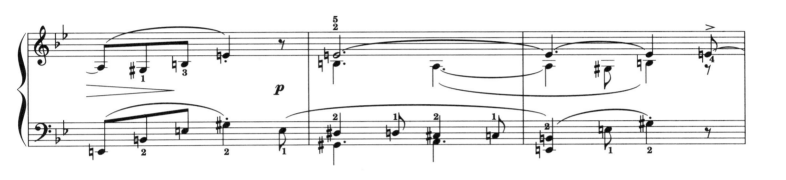

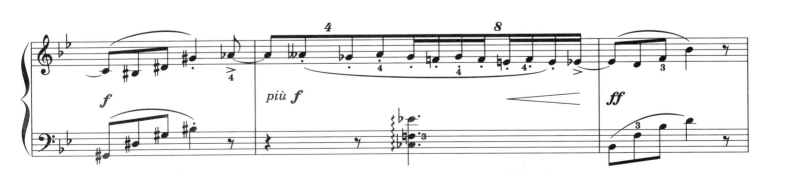

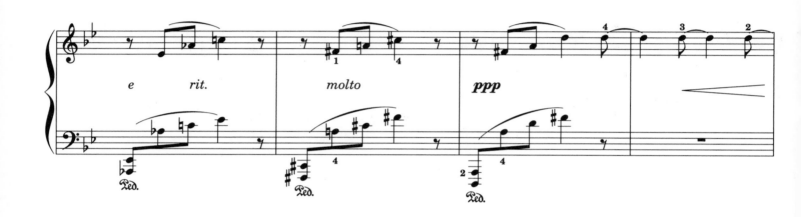

Tempo I

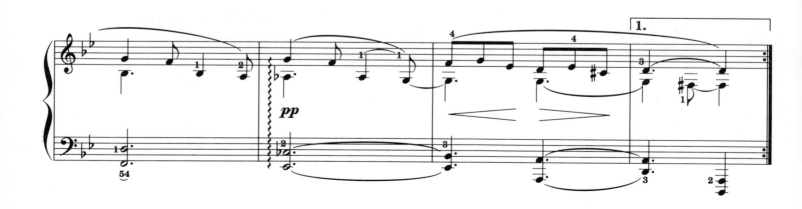

Solvejg's Song
from Peer Gynt Suite No.2

Edvard Grieg

Waltz
from Lyric Pieces, Op.12

Edvard Grieg

Allegro moderato

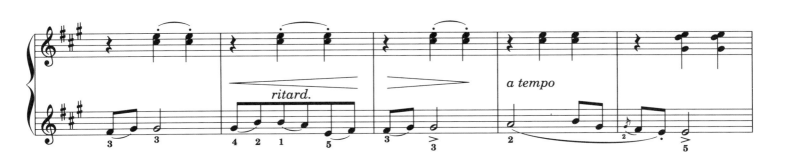

64